SHUFFLE
(Introducing—
Anime Titles)
Joseph Simas

THE BODILY PRESS
AMHERST, MA

Shuffle (Introducing—Anime Titles)

Copyright © 2026 Joseph Simas

All rights reserved. Except for brief passages quoted for usage in online or print sources (e.g. newspaper, magazine, podcast), no part of this book may be reproduced in any form or by any means, electronic or mechanical, including photocopying and recording, or by any information storage and retrieval system, without permission in writing from the publisher.

ISBN: 978-1-971551-01-2

This book is set in Garamond Premier Pro and LTC Kennerley Pro.
Book design and layout by Eliot Cardinaux and Joseph Simas.

Cover images:
Front: NASA/GSFC, MODIS Rapid Response Team,
Jacques Descloitres, Low pressure system over Iceland, 2003.
Back: Tule Fog in Bakersfield
https://en.wikipedia.org/wiki/Tule_fog

Bodily Press logo designed by Katya Popova.

THE BODILY PRESS
www.bodilypress.com
@thebodilypress

ACKNOWLEDGMENTS

Many thanks to editors Harley Healy & Yates Cessna for publishing the first version of the title play—"Shuffle (for Michael)"—in their newsprint magazine *thruline #3*. The author has posted versions of parts of *Shuffle (Introducing—Anime Titles)* on Facebook. Here the author would like to express his special thanks to Carla Harryman in whose Ypsilanti study-home a part of this book was first read before a gathering of students and poets; to guest curator Steve Dickison for his invitation to read at the celebrated unnamed weekly series at Tamarack in Oakland; to Ivan Sokolov for his early translation and *Telegram* publication in Russian of a key part of *Shuffle* . . . ; and, finally, to Michael Schuffler without whose assiduous readings and conversations this book would not be as it is.

SHUFFLE
*(Introducing—
Anime Titles)*

"And on the table there is an elegant syntax—
of confused heteroalphabet, grammatically
wrong wildflowers, as though all the preschool
forms of vegetative nature were coalescing
into a pleothonic anthology poem."

—Osip Mandelstam
from *Journey to Armenia*
(translation, Clarence Brown)

WHAT ABOUT ME

It is slow acting

It is familiar

It is gravity on rails

Splitting

Laughter comes over it

It bares its few teeth

Someone watches it

It summons a contradiction of decay and anger

A kindness

Set in motion

It lifts a lonely hand

It points a finger

AIRBORNE AND FEATHERING

Mirror a time unfit to mirror

One leans away feebly

Inclines up close

Upon a divisible shelf

Casts a faint shadow print

Injury aslant
Folds lightly bouncing off slope
At face value
It flails at sense
It is a bright twinkle in the eye
One long ecstatic emergency
It is unrelenting
Silken sheets creeping up face
Letters cascading
It is an enveloping almost
It is a ruthless curtain study
It means by scattering proof
It means a heart askew
Body flat out on its sensuous back
Dead eyes fixed on heaven
Blank stare pulls itself up
Zombies on the loose
In the two-dimensional worlds
Call them paper ghosts
Call them tree spirits on screen
Shroud kodama syllables click click
Surfaces widely spreading
Outward whoosh glare
Whoops a blanket flutter
Starry fluorescence
In tired old bones bending

Indexed and referenced
Nearly personal at cross purposes
Lights on inbound pulse
Ceiling receding
Reading between breaths
Between thighs
Threads of veined fabric
Mesh of life pillowed expanse
It is all choked up
It is shunted by angst
Spewed triangles of anger
Disorder patterns throughout
Indwelling ribbon sequins
Neither hem nor button
Lodged in lower abdomen
Amid draperies
A final keepsake
And from these threadbare lines a hinge
An animated hiss and mortal kiss
Almost a melting gift
It twitches it quivers
In volleys of chaotic growth
It alters taut seams
It squirms through
It screams
Arrows

AND WHAT ABOUT ANIME TITLES

It is wanting honey around
Where swarms verb
It drips it oozes
It is I that follows
And soothsayers
In a future that will not come
It will not be yet
It is a passion it unfolds
And a curse
It is one around about
What a sticky situation
It is wanting to go back
Lost in the thick of it
It is waiting
For a warning sign
It is a rising up
What a mess
And it cannot go back
It is a foreseeable disaster
It is a minefield of bad faith
It is an unruly kind
It is a hand
In a filthy pot
It is a persimmon bleeding

How symbolic it is and how bloody fruity
How sense-confused
It is wanting succor
In the form of it
In this passing by
It is a conflation of contingencies
A moving
It is an unthing
Vibrations cough inside it
It is a high doughnut warp
Peering out
It is an exhibition
It images it rolls it means
About a turning
About a vacuum
It is glass trapped in spirit
Whereabouts known
And unknown
Bodies in war zones missing
And found
What a sad plight
It is wanting and waiting
Poring over questions
Fattened and sickly
Oozing life
Ripe still

A LAND THAT MAKES A HEART SKIP A BEAT

It is alive and kicking in a tin
In expansive throes
It is an oceanic explosion
An astral head on a chopping block
It is a widowmaker on ice
It is a body riddled
It is a soul ever so pure
It is deafening
It is a crashing wave

It is a sound long after
Silence my little love sardine
It is unticking
It is reeling out
It is laughing in high spirals
It is all over the place
It is homing in
Down familiar paths
Of breadcrumbs and blood
Back of it a flight
It sits on high
Behind a ridge
It swoops down
To pristine beach
Weds river silt to desert
In a valley of circuits
It is a dwelling place
A code redirects
It starts its way over
Elsewhere familiar
It gives pause
It is one wrong turn
It is neither button
It is thrown off guard
It is blown sky high
Its state leaves my mouth

THE DEATH DRAFT OF A PAGE

The children as evidence

Switching of genres

Of happy and mad—mad in rage

Happy beyond all belief

Just listen to all of them laughing

Before convictions

Listen to the chaos of sincerity

Playing dead

Standing up and running away

It is quiet here at night. Though never this quiet, and rarely as still. After midnight the highway traffic driving alongside the main rail artery can often be heard in dreams, and our seaside cottage is close enough to feel the tremors of long and heavy freight trains as they pass. Thought is darker and stiller than pitch. A little over one beat per second, a tone a little over one thousandfold, persistent and damning. It will begin to hurt as it rises higher and higher. A distant rumble from afar, a supply truck perhaps or a convoy of military vehicles. Now gone, like distant thunder. Still again and dark and rather eerie—missing voices, inner sound. People too are altered here, quieter, and darker, confused somewhat, and out of place. Their smiles are less rustic, their laughter less verdant, their greetings less kind and generous. No wind amid the trees, no distant howling or owl song, car traffic quiet in town and nearby settlements. One of the four a.m. trains should be passing soon. Perhaps one will awake to the report. The dog has received no stray visitors. No mice scurrying about. Time must still be passing. What is happening over there, or there, or there a few thousand kilometers away, and does the quiet extend to other parts of the distanter world. Sound of a beating heart while reading personal accounts of people holed up in rundown houses and tenements. How differently the quiet moves this silence, this stillness, this lack of outside. What else is there to make sense of—what one is sounding now. Nothing measurable, nothing identifiable, but noisier images, more chaotic images. No train. The sea is still. No moon, no fireworks, no one knocking at the door. Just yet.

When one has nothing to say
Yet still a mind to say it
One might as well give up
And address the stars again
Or return to bed and sleep
And start writing then
As day is broken, and night long past
An ear to the wise is listening
That is the cinema in one's head
And the symphony at one's feet
While in the belly of the beast
Memories and monsters commingle
Absurd laughter erupts in fits and starts
Of weeping, thoughts stumble
Upon fruits of repressed desire
And readings passed down
So many heads and pages turned
That leave nothing behind
But what remains to be said

At the slip, if it is a place, though one cannot say
For certain where to find it
By north or south, in order or disorder, or there
At the very thought of your touch
Then the hand rests
For an impossibly brief instant
Attentive to the wind
A state shared by many bodies, but separate
Waiting for a sign
Where to look next, left or right
How to move, and precisely on what path
Knowing as a hand does
Which others elsewhere may also be considering
That any move in any direction at all
Will suddenly alter its position

Incipit, or Opening

Wake up to shortness of breath and incomplete proposition, dry mouth, faint sound of radio announcer, neighboring occupants, sunlight through the corner window curtain, today is an object-filled world—ideas, bodies, lands, steam, matter, space—spongy. One feels almost fine but breathing is clumsy, heartbeat uneven. One is overly aware of a lag from restless sleep, liquid dreams gone, recall news from yesterday, that too is real, half forgotten. Wished away, tethered still. Hand down between thighs. Nothing quite hurts. Eros is lacking, cloying though. Heroes, personalities, idols, enough of all that. Close the eyes, return to sleep, open wide, stare at ray of light through window, the dust, blink. Recall the news. War is sincerely the beginning to never ending—denials, rationales, euphemisms lie in wait. Nowhere to turn, one must leave again, one must breathe, deeper, move now, the whole body in mind, like a carnage, luggage trailing behind.

One should be a formalist about the matter. One is tired of confessional, weary of personality. War is formal.
Formal appears to last. Salute.
Formal is militaristic.
Military is a mountain with a pyramid inside.
Inside the pyramid
God is formal. God is missing.
There will be many false words.
Construct truths from them.

SHUFFLE

(A Reader Play, for Michael Schuffler)

ACT ONE

An open stage, black floor and backdrop screen.
Character on the edge of stage, stage right.
(In an aside, speaking silently to oneself, one repeated line, indistinct.)
Character visibly soft, fully covered in drapery.
Backdrop image—creamy light brown skin (e.g. lower back or nape of neck).
Enter Character, in an awkward choreographed walk, stage right to left.
Stop center stage, at slight angle, back to audience.
Light and shadow.
Speaking out.
One line, from indistinct to familiar sound of words, though not "natural speech."
(Offstage Voice)—Found word now start,
announcing word myself.
Character folds into drapery, rests immobile.
Fuzzy halo of hoarfrost appears around
Character silhouette.
Hoarfrost halo fades to black.
Dark shape of Character faintly visible.

Intentionally dreaming into an abstract field of writing—memory, character, space all tending toward the familiar, resulting in an odd but simple narrative construct. A story built from desire, formal manipulation of measures (and combinations of same) of time and space, and commonplace yet infinitely distinct and altering constructed experience. Recounting, so to speak, what one cannot say, what one has not done. But—not what if, nor what might have been. So the narration builds from a verbal momentum, events in which all is language and its silences. Since language already contains all possible reference, it precedes experience: one may choose to look back, thinking that this gives one the names to say how it was, but such returning is rather a search for experience that is already named, and which, if the writing comes into its own, then becomes a novel form of thought, sensation, and again, to speak generally, experience that is proper to language. One then becomes a person again.

SHUFFLE

ACT TWO

Backdrop photo of pool of clear water from above.
Same photo becomes moving image—pane of glass cracks, shatters in pool.
Image off.
Hoarfrost halo around dark shape of
Character lights up.
Enter Full-length Mirror, stage left to right.
Mirror rolls to a stop in front of draped
Character, facing audience.
Mirror swivels slowly to face Character.
Mirror image and Character are distorted abstractions.
Shapes are illusions.
(Offstage Voice)—Found word in mouth fuzzy, feeling word.
Hoarfrost halo fades into thin wisps of hair, in a breeze.
Character shape and Mirror shape move independently.
They merge into crude cloaked figures, facing backdrop.
Bright eyes open wide in the back of their heads.
Backdrop sudden flash matches general brightness.
All lights out.

In the offhand weather of annihilation, when one must shut the book down, when one stops reading, three kids, each under a dusty sheet in a room desolate of sound, two of them sleeping in silence, a mute silence before words are formed, before their waiting turns on fear, the other motionless at the turn of a page, its breath-fall against its sequel, a flutter simultaneous with the click of an old flashlight, its dull glow snuffed out as the bedroom door opens onto a dark silhouette, an image set against a pitch black ground that skews the picture out of perspective—pictures of reality end abruptly, the door shuts, the light hits the page, and one is caught up again in another world, a safer refuge it seems, but it is not: two heaps of dust, one heap of light, a simulacrum resumed, the elder watching over in kaddish, rewriting an improved version of events through the flawed text, rereading one letter at a time, being wanted over there, in motion such as turning—as the sky falls, and eyelids drop, and in these common words, story gets lost, language pales in the fire of the page, and the bodies that once were are put to rest.

SHUFFLE

ACT THREE

Dim general light of sunrise.
Character and Full-length Mirror
same positions as above, without eyes.
Ultra-slow sky-blue strobe light on backdrop.
Character Figure and Mirroring Figure turn in sync
with strobe light to face audience.
(The two Figures look almost identical.)
Drapery cloaks fall to the floor.
Two faceless Androgynous Figures stand tall, dressed head
to toe in sheer earthen-colored djellabas.
(Offstage Voice)—Word curls into word before crawling.
Sky-blue strobe light on backdrop increases rate.
Sounds of heartbeats in sync quicken.
Backdrop turns into solid image of sky-blue sky.
Cumulus clouds fade into backdrop.
Figures turn their backs to one another.
General daylight grows darker.
Clouds grow menacing.
Heartbeats slip out of sync, volume grows louder.
Sound of distant thunder.
Sound of incipient rain.
Figures exit, walking slowly away from one another.
Immersive thunder, heartbeats.
Downpour.
Darkness.

I walked through a little boy on the beach today. Suddenly there he stood, square in my path, unfazed, looking out at the waves, and I passed impossibly through him without hesitation, though in retrospect concerned somewhat, whether he had in fact been there or I had done something terribly wrong. But it was nothing of the sort; there he stood, indifferent to my presence, a real live boy of around eight or nine and, as sure as day, planted there between his feet one could clearly make out my footprint in the wet sand. How else to behave but to carry on my way. A double exposure of a banal scene—a precise moment shared in the same spot just as perfectly as a mirror image. The boy had nothing to say. He continued to gaze undisturbed at the foggy horizon. In fact nothing, no one had been disturbed. I moved along slowly, folding through the event most naturally. The ocean waves, for that matter, continued their raucous ebb and flow. Waning sunlight illuminated the wall of dissipating fog on the horizon. Turning away at a slight angle toward the water I felt the pull of the tide grow and the incoming waves crashing just below my knees. I looked back. The boy was still there, a few other adults nearby, a few dogs running around. Hardly unusual for a walk on the beach. A wide veil of mist seaward shimmered, drifting closer.

Silence could be the truer way. Perhaps I should dwell in my office, design a useful artifice, sit there and for hour upon hour pretend to compose, look at the walls and listen to what they have to say, then start all over again and feign to tell what I cannot tell, and claim to tell what cannot be told. Then again, perhaps this is precisely what there is to say, and as you read these words I write, I skip and play behind you, a mere shadow of myself, merry and contrite.

I wind a thread around my finger and snap it. I watch her in a mirrored chamber grasp her finger and grimace. There, across from me, she sits, in dark water. Her open hand is webbed; it glides through the wispy flora toward me. It is a painted chamber where I sit, needle in one hand, spool in the other. There is a dividing glass between us. It clouds form. Blood trickles into blue water. Across the frame tears flow.

One—a figure behind a tiny desk, scribbling frantically. Two—before cramping—a messy object spills onto paper. On a virgin canvas—flowers and mines grow there. Seated subject nearby bangs head on table. Three—a child sticks hand in mouth on purpose. Because doing so is fun. It gags the process. It is tilling and sowing. Words piled all around—drowning out sound—heaps of surplus verbiage symbols downstream from scattered limbs blood trickles. Ink forming awkward letters into giddy epiphanies. Idiot child cups ear to eloquent belly. Silence before heartbeat— no rest. Only—a face appears from behind, blurred and heavy—catching breath. Foreign mass without features swims across winds down. Scribbling unravels in reverse slow motion. Stubby index finger of child draws circles on big belly. It is tickling. It is sensational joy fraught with pain. It is so much more than one has been taught. There is more horror to it than meets the eye.

. . . scribbling that does not tend toward order scribbling memories that everyone has had scribbling to snuff out little ones scribbling winds rains snows that cancel lost memories that return to haunt them scribbling all big people that try to snuff them out all big people that fill up with ghosts scribbling all big people to ward off trauma scribbling to forget about birth scribbling to learn more about ghosts that do not fear dying scribbling little ones that do not care that come and go scribbling little ghosts that linger at their shoulder little ghosts that breathe into their ear scribbling one cannot hear scribbling figures that breathe louder and louder one hears only oneself breathe . . .

Subject—a child like a ghost a child is never sitting still. One scribbles on wall another inside back of skull another on window another on table. All folded papers go up in flames. All words are folded and little fingers are folded symbols pointing these things come and go and fly like little ghosts come and go breathing grows frantic. Everywhere scribbling starts and stops it is manifold it disappears and reappears. It follows lines of obedient little ones piles of books on folded shoulders blood runs downstream staining little paper boats as they sink.

WHAT ABOUT US

It is together

It is up in arms

It is a turn away

In a cup

A glitch

Its gaze clockwise

A flutter event

It is burning paper

Gauze stuff fog stuff

Its mouth is triangular

It puffs and poofs

It is dust swept

It is kin

It murmurs *sh— sh—*

It is wretched

A sweet stench

A whiff of it

Stringy or icky

It is kinder

It is velocity of desire

At a standstill

It is wanting body

Its hollow scream

Holler holler

HOW LIKE THEM

It is all mirrored

It is all that is seen

It is slightly off

It is as close as they come

It is hunted

It is wanting the hunter

It is hurt

It haunts a better way

It is wanting proximity

It is closing in

It is both at once

It is consonant

It is preyed upon

It feeds on distance

It moves in for the kill

VERY DEEP PIT

It is present indifference

It is gangly dug

Grown tall hunched over

Risen to be folded

It is a rough fabric

It is an earthen cloak

It is matted clay

Minerals and mulch

It is unbinding light

Blank to the third eye

It is dark within

Stage lights on

A body

It envelops trembles

It is propped on that hat

It is snake emblem

It is rind or bark

It is easy to peel

It is a soft edible creature

It is writhing

It sways as a tree or a building

It is a collective gasp

It is a veil that slowly falls

In clotted rivulets

It wriggles beneath

TRACKING FOOTSTEPS

It is an escapade

In an hourglass

Periodically ticking

It is a strong gale

In a puff of ashes

It falls like powder
It falls from scattered remains
And rises a ballerina
It digs and twirls
It summons hailstones
From a grain of sand
A mirror grain and a phantom grain
It is a neck
In locks of hair
It stings desire and dust
Clicking hard heels
Mixing drinks and categories
It is daintily thus
In between sand and glass
Time caught
In first things
In warm damp places
It is this cry or that
It comes without sensation
Without value
A dime song perhaps
A cry and cries
An escape path
Universal and void
From womb
It takes place

STRANGE ANIMAL

Plush toy will it be mine

Baby totem

It is alive

Once it was

Twice not

Vision far beyond

A blinding illustration

Picture is sun

Monkey will it be plush totem

A child keeper minds it

It is monkey soul

Plush paint will it be solution

It is an ocean bath

It is full up

Solution once heavy lotion

Golem mud bath

It slips inside its robe

Slowly disappears

Word will cover

It is hard shell

Empty mollusk

Word will not ever

In tunnel time

It simply moves things

That moves us

CARTOON ROOM

PLAYERS
Adult Voice
Youngster

The stage is divided into two equal parts. Stage right: An open lab with a mock-up of a generic bedroom—bed, desk, chair, pile of boxes of different colors. Surveillance cameras are placed in the four corners of the lab. Stage left: A large window onto a control booth furnished with audiovisual recording devices, emergency protocol information signs, first-aid equipment—two empty chairs and a long table.

ADULT VOICE (soothing): *Weirdos grow on you. They do things to you. Many say weirdos look psycho goofy with messed up eyes. They stare at you with those sick eyes. The taboo words scare those who use them because in them one often sees oneself, or that terrible part of oneself one hides from within. The weirdos bewitch you with jewels in their skulls and tag along behind you. Waiting in costumes. Waiting. Weirdos tear up to sadly weep and in the next minute smile crooked smiles and scream and holler. Weirdos are sick scary. They touch you and want you to touch them. To hold them. They act happy until you look away for just a second and they bite your ear and scratch your face. That is how they are. That is why you are so afraid of them.*

YOUNGSTER is sitting on bed in lab, hands out, alone, playing patty cakes with an invisible friend. Youngster is hyper-ventilating, working up to a frenetic slap-happy pace, and looking around with quick paranoid jerks of the head. Soothing voice interrupts Youngster who stops moving and gasps to catch breath.

There is no worry, do not hurry. There is no worry, do not hurry. There is no worry, do not hurry. We have all the time in the world. In this world and in the next. In this world and in the next. There is nothing to fear. In this world and in the next. Now tell me how the weirdos grow on you. Wait until you are ready. Do not hurry. We have all the time in the world. In this world and in the next.

Youngster listens intently, stares vacantly straight ahead.

Weirdos come from before. When everything was void and dark. They come from the first darkness. That one in which you were there and not yet there. They know who you are already, they are part of you, hiding inside you.

In a flash, Youngster is on all fours in a tense and focused stance, poised between absolute stillness and quick bounding attack. Youngster's silent and invisible counterpart appears to have vanished. Youngster is focused on a faraway sight.

This has been very instructive. Thank you. That is all for today. You are free to do as you please. Your sleep is sound and in darkness your eyes are shining jewels. Your eyes are shining jewels. The light is in your dreams. Everything is calm in the middle of the night.

Simultaneously a door opens in the lab and in the control room. Behind each door a long vanishing line of what appear to be standing stick-figures (no one can tell why or how many).

ENTER INTRODUCING BOTH

An observer, in hiding, standing in front of a mirror—being oneself, being good, hiding in plain sight—remarks to no one in particular, from the mirror, *Go see what happens*. Enter Both, the observer, exiting from the mirror, having once stood in the wings—being oneself, being good—stepping forth into the open space, now standing there, waiting, listening, perhaps bleeding.

Again. Enter Both, from the mirror out into the open, beside oneself, shadowing nearly—alone yet—an innocent bystander next to a sleeping absence, slowly bleeding out.

Nonchalant, like death, alone there, between several mirroring figures—aping one another—there Both stands, a shade of sorts, hiding in plain sight, self-conscious.

Thereafter trapped in self-circus-hell with occasional moments of complete abandon, sleeping perhaps, pulse undivided—waiting, listening, floating above for distant contact. Both trade places on and off in thunderclouds of abrasive attention to detail. Both, swaddled in cloth of pomp and circumstance, wrapped in tinfoil, begin the ancient anarchic breathing patterns, inner stutters, false starts, irrational fits of laughter. Doubt—start contact—allowing engagement, observation, disparate flight, in union as in slumber. Doubt—follow the signs—star-gazing with chimeras in stellar sleep, pitch darkness drawing in light. Doubt—smile indulgently—grand selfie-envy, inclined to obsessive mood disorders. Doubt—embrace the absurd—reading telltale facial signs, twitches, perspiration. Doubt—resist hesitation—now removed and calm, now torn and scattered. Doubt—move in close—doubled-over, syncopated, neurotic, superfluous. Doubt—end abandoned—alone and bleeding, in this obscure clearing, vast and desolate.

Some say a sign then, others an image. Paranoia gives way to complex primal emotion, an infant being comes to life—from fluid units and crossings—a helpless symbol, an animated creepy thing, an elemental form, more or less cute, symmetrical, fishily so, amphibian-like, shadowy—designed to traverse dimensions. Species crossing—magnificent and meaningful. Creatures all and purposes alike under the blazing furnace of the sun.

Incessant innocence of birth, of names for being here, of yearning for animus, flesh-spirit, rebirth, a name alone with no discernible identity, no complementary lasting image. Not yet. Both—its screen time only now, light traces upon present tense, and even as time restricts, it recurs, ongoing and perpetual. A sign daubed in a cave, a crude diffraction, a name that comes to signify, that comes to return—a show of purpose for oneself, one who is whole and unaware, who doubts no more, who reciprocates.

Lost in the wings, behind the curtains, elsewhere. Both—returning over and over, desirable again, cherished, and protected—mirrored askance, wanting, ongoing—in the same place as before.

Pictures flash by—faces!

No one else can see them.

Almost intimate familiar voices.

Back here, back here.

Over and over.

Symmetry fails.

Dark turmoil as raging fire—eyes turn red, lawn goes up in smoke, sky goes bright with blood, laughter becomes screaming—no room for flight—a world turned inside-out, from underneath and all around, silence then, nearly, Both, at a loss for place, helpless, side by side, still wanting, waiting.

Suddenly hot air surges into cold lungs. And Both revive one in the other.

No telling how.

Pictures flash by—places!

Experience goes on and on—a single almighty breath, repeated ad infinitum, on after and before, in this or that direction—one forgets—to a precise location, somewhere almost familiar. Eventually, one moves—as if swayed by infinitesimal differences. Introducing is being here before.

Both enter, stumble around for a spell, trip, fall face down, flat out, rise to their knees, awkwardly stand, coughing up sand. Both struggles to speak. Two distinct tones sound out. The first sharp and clear, the second hoarse and wheezy. Both address a solitary self, deceptively simple and natural.

Both as one. Memory is itching for it.

Interiors! Vertiginous landscapes!

Pictures flash by—objects!

Both divide and interlace, turn head away and around to assume another fleshy, anomalous figure in motion. Animal of human fold—bewildered, infantile, androgynous, beastly, many, gorgeous.

Pictures flash by—reflections!

All moving all about.

Both remain silent and alert. Out there—a flame like a faulty fluorescent tube—focus wobbles as the light falls. The trouble—distress—in such a state—gasping—of panic—lure Both in. Bizarre breathing—Both reach out, stab really, over and over, poking, tearing, burning with abandon. No one can see them!

Pictures flash by—trees! these trees!

A dark wood lit by a candle at dusk. Slow rising winds blend into two-tone sound of breathing. Candle bleeds out. Wind and breath intertwine. Anxiety which had begun its increase fades.

And is gone.

In a heartbeat, being there—nowhere else—Both whisper, in a heartbeat, at long last.

Both continue standing there, wishing to forget all over again, lapsing on and on—to end up here. Breathless, bleeding—emptiness, its design everywhere, gone for good.

At the break of a clouding of planes, lapse of place, time to see, a crossing over, Both turn to leave, walks through the mirror.

Such errant oddities—eclipse two as one—their measures meaningless in any other setting. Behind the main curtain another drops, seen only on the back side, which is identical to the front, though uncannily out of this world, so Both speak at odds to one another.

NERVES GONE HAYWIRE

Luckily history has forgotten

An unwanted child

There were documents

And an education

Forged from four mistaken identities

Face of human being

Face of roaming sea creature

Face of spector

Face of eagle slowly diving

In a perpetual spin

Two intersecting discs

Mystical experiences

Soon enough just another little kid

All by his lonesome

IT WAS A SKY MACHINATION THAT FELL

An outer edge amid dull borders
Of solitude in this alone case
A fluid just as it is in this state
Put into words that fit just right
Conserved in jars and poured from jars
Poetry and honey have this in common
Jars and words contain the secrets
Wanted and unwanted sweet stickiness
Ooze preserved and spilled
Fade to words and sugar-pane glass
It is dry and lonely
It is foggy out there sand and snow
It is as brittle as a cracker
Poetry and honey have nothing in common
Words and jars and people are lonely

IT IS NAMED AFTER THAT MYTH

It is a game of peek-a-boo

In the court of philosophers

It heads straight for the corner

Turns back flush to the wall

Pulls out a bag of tricks

It turns and returns

It is a windmill

On paper it reads whoosh

It is a flying body

Mangled in parts

It flails about *sans raison*

Inside a stone head

Hard seeds of fruit for eyes

Jagged iron teeth

Whoosh

Its hat is a wicker basket

Its nose and ears are hearsay

By the time I had questioned my awareness of the tree, this one in particular, walking past it, not being familiar enough with its species to name it, it became apparent that what mattered at the moment was the high canopy above, in effect the tree's peculiar crown and its mangled branches that had made me stop, turn back, and look up beyond to see the dark clouds forming through its broad leaves. Before the depiction of leaf and cloud had blurred and turned splotchy, I recall projecting an image of late autumn that was still a few months away while being distracted by the noise of traffic along the beach highway masking the sound of waves—a curtain of dark fog slipped between sound and noise spread wide and high all of a sudden my hearing skipped a few beats I could no longer tell where I stood dizzy and afraid I lunged toward the trunk of the tree. One does not know what to make of a man alone and unconscious in a park these days. Now it seemed that I, who had become a strange player of myself, shied away from story and held fast to a painterly vertigo that had twirled me upright, staring upward, lost in a vision assembled at that instant for my eyes only. It turns out that one ends up speaking to oneself, to no one else in particular, saying little if anything worth repeating. Tethered to the moment, in the eye of the crown spinning round and round, spilling colors and motion, I grew more and more ill and faint of heart. It seemed likely that I would soon fall, one does eventually, yet I determined to stand tall, leaning tethered mind to tree, becoming one circuitous stage so to speak. Experience as conduit flowing down through crown, holding on for dear life to the neck of this twisting hourglass—that which spirals, selects, and counts the events that end up here as a picture storm. Dizzy inner stage—two quasi-voices attempt to dialogue, it is what thinking wants to do, but can't—what one wishes to put into words is what one is already saying. Telling is the base content of ground, ground defines tree, tree reaches out to canopy. Just so the whole process results in a verbal crown, a monologue hearing oneself fall on an empty stage, no one else around.

Journal entry. A group of sham military and intel handlers convene at the border town of X in ragtag uniforms and shady insignia. I know because my employer at the time was a member of one of the visiting groups, a covertly funded crew of thugs, investors, local opportunists, not to mention wannabe psychics and shamans. Motley cohorts of spiritual advisors and seers—ex-models and athletes, fallen Orthodox nuns, *nouveaux riches*, and foreign nationals appeared like clouds at various checkpoints, baffling and bribing or seducing local national officials. The truth is no one belongs here. Like so many small border towns all over the world the lines one sees on maps and official documents are invisible and subject to all manners of crossing. Everyone acting important wears a partial uniform. Doors and passages are coded, penetrable sieves. This has not always been the case. Everyone has a so-called rank or so-called title. Cut-off points—arbitrary stations of temporary control on both sides are manned by young recruits and old volunteers. Nearly all soldiers, officers, and muscle on both sides are men wearing a variety of uniforms: military, urban camp, plain clothes, sporting, city fashion, camouflage, tribal furs, vogue, and leather goods. Women occupy mostly hidden or obscured roles essential to the ongoing social push for survival of the greatest number. In these early stages of war, males are predominant, in your face, all-powerful, exceptions be damned. The men travel in groups and fondle one another with deep care and affection—they look at and after each other even more caringly than they track down and kill their enemies. Cowardice is being possessed by an irrational fear of words. Cowards know that at whatever cost one must never entertain the possibility that words could be the source of all that is right in this world. Wishful thinking—words could lead to mutual acceptance, if not understanding. Cowards are deeply troubled, easily triggered men with hearts as deep as shallow graves.

Infiltrators who cross over in the early days are stopped at numerous checkpoints to be reminded of their station in life. Forget your name, soldier. Do not speak to your enemy, coward. You are a knife and a gun and a bomb. Use yourself and your brother in that order. In silence sneak up from behind and slit the throat of all vile talk. At a distance aim to let loose a single fatal cry of victory. In the midst of panic unleash a deafening blow of rage.

Unseen, near the night camps, the witches, the healers, and the spiritual con artists gather in circles of prayer and vicious gossip.

Doomsday looms. Motherland is a bitch. Everyone wants a piece of her.

One, along the shore, not looking at an other, naturally, and the other, at water's edge, both heading toward a creature in common, obliquely walking toward one another, shadowing, yet also drifting apart, eyes running wild, suspended in a sleight of hand by sensual surprise, instantaneous, instantly fleeting, slant and smiling—innocent deception! And one is suddenly caught up in odd anatomy, in longing, in unabashed energy, flesh against a melting expanse of winter yet, in a word red, in a word beautiful, a new spring sun, harsh against an icy desert of blinding whiteness, a shallow lake, still frozen over, crackling here and there, fissuring, and a shadow figure's long mythical hair, an invitation—blushing darkness, perhaps—and laughter belonging to another time and place. A roaring drone of cargo planes above does not spoil the horizon. No one says the real word for it—everything happens in fits and starts, everywhere, composed of little corners, of hideaways, of designated safe spots. Nowhere is the best place of all, that's where nothing ever happens. One says, I'm going nowhere, I'm going far away, I'm falling to pieces.

Another moment passes, another yet to come. In the stillness of which an animal adjacent to mind grows, one has no clue, it's all a personal sideshow, a wound-up attraction of visceral maneuvering, both unpredictable and disordered. One does not pause or feign to pose, does not allow others to master, nor even pretend to care about their presence. One longs to—but cannot. Who might as well have been walking on all fours, in a free, now menacing now pathetic state—every bit as stray as a streetwise dog eluding capture. All of a sudden one is displaced, found not knowing to whom one belongs, where one animal transverses shadow paths with another. In constant, implacable fear, in surging impulse between moral spring and mortal coil.

A little boy sees a dog from afar, beckons, unafraid until too late, until contact, startled then, but knowing still in nervous connection, in tether that does not break, that adapts to each touch, at each test. Creature comes to wrap around and caress, to intervene, to entangle. In this animal embrace, a mother does not waver. Bringing stranger and creature into her fold.

From a distance, an encroaching patrol snarls at the scene, approaches upright in uniform complicity with unthinking obedience. *Your papers, madam!* To the other, *You there! Stay still!*

She knows the words by heart. She understands their inevitable outcome. She sees a split-second into the future. Her act now a shadow heartbeat, convulsive, in a vacuum, a resounding, stunned suck of all sound. No before time, none after.

The boy knows not to disturb the silence. The dog knows. It barely whimpers. It moves in close.

Mother regains balance, ears still ringing. *You must hurry now*, she cries.

Fragments prevail. Shrapnel prevails over word as mind boggles, how distort wraps
around, one fails to attain composure,
flags down creature and I
as orders must. As controllers count every last one of us.

Creature and I must sync our racing hearts down the main path. In someone else's conflict, a warring in our own skies, and in our own selves.

Creature and I must account for failure to reason, to compassion, to unrot, to word,
to unstain, to disobey,
as only a good one would,
as so many are unable.
Old men—submissive to roles,
absurdly inconsequential
to creature energies. Men fashioned by state, ruled by base ideologies, slavish obedience
to righteous ill.

Oh, I know I try to say too much, words arise in embarrassment, and in shame.
Our cheap makeup of social norms
deadens, trips over idols,
analyzing and observing them in misplaced worship.

Out of the blue comes a whimsical tune. A whistle. An Old Figure on the road.

How's life?—so goes the story, says he.

It's curtains, everywhere curtains, so they say! How's the sky for you, stranger? Ah, even the sky is tainted. Tell me the truth, dear enemy—is this not still a patch of paradise? Who in these parts suspects you? They won't hear a word from me!

Creature and I look up at the harsh sun, then again at the shadows below.

WHAT MY EYES DO, SAID PROUST

In the moment is
To take a photograph
My eyes
My ellipsis reading Proust
Sees the photograph develop in reverse
On the move
After it has been taken away
So to speak
What reading means

**BEING AFRAID TO ABUSE THE WORDS
THAT DISTURB ME**
The words within words
And words that in flesh have none to speak of
Still I have a play and yet another play
The name is a sleight of hand
Look here
One needs to escape the fear of it all
I am so sorry to have been afraid
This is the way fits and starts must go
When I forget how to speak
I can hear myself talking
What one must say one cannot truly repeat
Now I forget you, and even memory itself, and faces
And all the places I have been
Have been erased by such episodic waves

THE COUGH

At each of the three pre-curtain bells, The Cough hesitates, pushes forth, expectorates, sounds almost faintly familiar, and remains invisible throughout.

Three women—one assumes—of whose proximity one is as yet unaware, hold evaporate. Their perfume is faint.

Interior space a huge empty concrete floor, propped to be a social arena soon, such as a ballroom or a grand salon.

Three handkerchiefs, slowly, randomly falling from on high above scene.

The Cough, naturally unseen, intimated as wheezing, as an incorporeal entity—it is already mingling.

Visual focus alternates between the three distantly floating handkerchiefs, approaching and growing apart as leaves in a sullen foggy wind.

Weeping is not a part of coughing, but torn, the lacrimae binds to another incipient cough as a singular cloud that will infiltrate the arriving crowd, still evaporate, yet moving in countless particles toward the gathering floor.

Charlotte Rampling appears coughing up blood in a dream by a former work colleague, Joseph Simas. One must have come this far, must have read one's own dark mind, far from everywhere, remembering almost nothing, fearing for another more than for oneself, as anyone who has known love has felt.

It has been time to speak up.

For the record, Joseph Simas met the movie star on only a handful of occasions, notably on the set of a motion picture for which he had been tasked with rewriting a number of substantial lines, in effect altering her role most decidedly. Due to a few fortuitous and casual off-set encounters, Joseph fancied being something of a welcome acquaintance to the renowned, indeed, iconic celebrity and, while no further relationship, friendship or other, developed between the two, their encounters were certainly cordial and light-hearted. She was most flattering toward him and, it seemed, genuinely amused by his outlier person. Still, it should be stated that the relationship between the celebrity and the poet remained solely professional, which is to say largely impersonal. Joseph has neither seen nor spoken to Charlotte Rampling for nearly 20 years. He would be most surprised to learn that he has crossed her mind at all since their brief collaboration. It goes without saying that Lady Rampling could have had nothing to do with the present story as it first manifested itself in Joseph's dream. While he has used her name without permission here, it must be stated that the character in his dream insisted upon it.

This is all because one wants to impersonate existence.

Charlotte Rampling's eyes are pure cinema. Joseph Simas, so-called, authored this play. Mind you, words are eyes and lights. All quiet. Words are pinches and blows and tickles.

Caresses

Curtains

Not so easy

Curtains gently part

Dim fish-eye view of scene

Hunger privation and atrocity
Terrify
You hear me

General coughing

Words and the lack of them
All the lovely all the lonely creatures
All the children here
Who will not rise
Because of us

Fade to black
Suddenly
All white

Now

        Curtains

INDEX OF ANIME TITLES & FIRST LINES

A LAND THAT MAKES A HEART SKIP A BEAT ... 15
AIRBORNE AND FEATHERING 10
An observer, in hiding, standing in front of a mirror (...) .. 46
An open stage, black floor and backdrop screen 25
AND WHAT ABOUT ANIME TITLES 13
ANIME TITLES 72
At each of the three pre-curtain bells (...) 64
At the slip, if it is a place, though one cannot say 21
Backdrop photo of pool of clear water from above 28
BEING AFRAID TO ABUSE THE WORDS
THAT DISTURB ME 63
By the time I had questioned my awareness of the tree ... 54
CARTOON ROOM 43
COUGH, THE 64
DEATH DRAFT OF A PAGE, THE 17
Dim general light of sunrise 31
ENTER INTRODUCING BOTH 46
HOW LIKE THEM 38
I walked through a little boy on the beach today 32
I wind a thread around my finger and snap it 34
In the offhand weather of annihilation 29
Incipit, or Opening 22
Intentionally dreaming into an abstract field of writing ... 26
Introducing is moving in between (...) 73

IT IS NAMED AFTER THAT MYTH	53
It is quiet here at night	18
IT WAS A SKY MACHINATION THAT FELL	52
Journal entry	56
NERVES GONE HAYWIRE	51
One—a figure behind a tiny desk, scribbling frantically	35
One, along the shore, not looking at an other	58
SHUFFLE — ACT ONE	24
SHUFFLE — ACT THREE	30
SHUFFLE — ACT TWO	27
Silence could be the truer way	33
STRANGE ANIMAL	42
The stage is divided into two equal parts	43
TRACKING FOOTSTEPS	40
VERY DEEP PIT	39
Wake up to shortness of breath (…)	22
WHAT ABOUT ME	9
WHAT ABOUT US	37
WHAT MY EYES DO, SAID PROUST	62
When one has nothing to say	20

ABOUT THE AUTHOR

Books by Joseph Simas include *Entire Days* (Burning Deck, 1985), *Sets* (TELS Press, 1986), *Aftersight* (Rue d'Aboukir, 1987), and *Kinderpart* (Paradigm Press, 1989).

His full-length manuscript, *Easy Lessons in Reading . . .* is published in French as *Premières leçons de lecture . . .* (Créaphis/Royaumont, 1996). He is translator, most notably, of *Mezza Voce* (Post-Apollo, 1988) by Anne-Marie Albiach.

His poetry is anthologized in *49+1 Nouveaux poètes américains* (Royaumont, 1991) and *Writing from the New Coast* (o·blēk, 1993). Numerous uncollected poems and translations are featured in *Temblor*, *Hambone*, *Po&sie*, *ACTS*, *Tyuonyi*, *Poetics Journal*, *Raddle Moon*, and Facebook to name a few sites.

He is founder and editor of Moving Letters Press (Paris, 1984-1990).

Anime Titles unwinds an "epic reader reel" that opens with *Shuffle . . .* (The Bodily Press, 2026), the book presently in your hands and at your mercy. Here follows

EPISODE ONE

of

ANIME TITLES

Introducing is moving in between and as far back as one can, recommencing, not that one could relive the same all over perhaps, though one might instead prefer to remove that which has been lost, or to find something, someone who likely knew, one with some kindred attachment, letting loose, reminder of and witness to each and every mistake, which one will then make a promise neither to lose again, though such a promise cannot be kept, nor to forget, which one cannot predict, nor to commit, the failure behind which weighs one down with shame, as such embarrassment grows so does one grow weary; and introducing is a similar utterance to that first sad cry which one cannot recall, though summoned it feigns remembrance as one returns to its familiar place, thus called because it has been named by others, there one is said to have done this or that for the very first time or, finding oneself in such a place much later, as witness to an other, one returns to it again as if fundamentally, as if there could be a second first time, and in this so-called familiar place, one feels a fondness for the objects, structures, and creatures present there, and this in turn becomes a longing familiarity, perhaps a lasting one, it allows one to move back and forth, an imperceptible moving through, to go in between, a longing derived from and with a real set of places, such as a state or being or having once been perhaps a whole world that has neither foreseeable nor predictable end or border;

and introducing is knowing that one or an other, that even oneself, so-called by others, is and has been there, is reaching out to meet prevailing circumstances, in the presence of other acting entities, as a reminder of states lost, and a desire of states to come; introducing then is moving in name, as name, toward naming and being named just as, simultaneous with, uncannily tethered to knowing in between as mind awakes to being there, as mind loses all sense of time, if only for an instant, or perhaps for hours on end, and what such a so-called state this is, a place, a person, a creature, a structure, an atmosphere, a motion, a physics of grace, an arrangement of furniture, a burst of energy, an architecture which one can tolerate only in the minutest of parts, for the briefest of moments, in the form of barely perceptible biochemical controls, all this largely unnamed while one keeps on knowingly naming others as best one can, for better or for worse, though always in motion toward a frightful end, while one pretends it is not necessarily so, how could it be, as instanter one is shown, wherefrom one cannot know farther than mind, either inner, outer, or surrounding, it seems all the same, and in this it imbues the psychophysical with a surplus weight, it depends upon the body to keep up, which, as far as one can tell, is, as in this case, a matter of substantive Grace, that is a form, a first name, which is a moving figure now, an immanence perhaps, which recognition has been bestowed upon one for no other reason than that one name works, as might the name of a laborer or a molecular exchange, through states of language, chatter above all else, wording so as to move easily and sweetly toward a mind of a most common makeup, yet both absolutely singular and distinct; it is in full motion then, in between word and sense, through the names one has been bestowed, that the mind grows, and knowledge grows, and even then that the anecdotal effects of a motion inscribed and shared among others may grow, and at that moment, by virtue of a felicitous and ongoing current through wobbling symbols mostly, through which one can sense how swiftly a second almost archaic name can be heard now emerging which one could neither have intended nor predicted, Felicity enters, as if it were to appear incarnate as representation that transports one back in time to a natural naming day which, while few can remember it, nearly all can attest to its occurrence, one lives with it oneself and soon it becomes an initiation, a selfhood perhaps, a mostly happy unselfconscious ritual if simply for the reason that one is called upon in between sign and stillness, to move, to sense one's own moving, and to move out toward others, in name only it seems desire, but which in all makes up one's whole mind, yet an infinitesimal part of a far greater nature, selfsame in many respects to other minds no doubt, but so vast that words within and without are infinitely numerous, and the knowledge derived from them will exponentially grow, and implode, which direction feeds all motion, rest, word bestowed, still only to keep on moving, to no end; please, move forth, even between sleep and its sister death, one mind within and without another, Grace from above, an air mind you, waters the ground to grow, the sun knocks off a breathing molecule that makes room for carbon to steel, the air one breathes suffocates in word for a slip between other matters, a second splits and comes out as a name for now altering states, moving at different speeds in opposite directions, from one mouth to an ear or eye, mind again in constant sensual flux, and one worries that it all ends, and one wants to get in the last word before it is too late, then slips down again to an abyssmal past, where name stays, and has more to say; Grace, please, why no more than life itself, and a possibility perhaps, without time or purpose, an ongoing comparison of same with same, how do Grace and Felicity differ, if as the whole time each moves alike, if in facets there is not one being that truly resembles another, a grandmother and her daughter, in a double-exposure snapshot, one, hovering between the two figures, pretending to remember who claims to have been there at such a time and place, and that is when one and all, never truly there, disappear for good, and shall not return, for one is called names, which is when a sensorial current in barely perceptible stop-motion flows and meanders, one could know it as remembers and forgets, in between alternating slips of senses, one could be said to establish mind, electric charge and connection, enter from all directions, entertain all elemental connections, isolate in such a so-called place and then, simply, begin all over again; and introducing naming, Grace enters slowly walking, shapeless yet, senseless, without image, motion continues to advance in its minute fits and starts, in between action and connection, naming is introducing Grace, this one knows, this one remembers and forgets, Grace exits, knowing her is then lingering, lingering fades, Grace passes quietly from left to right, these words her only image, growing thus and effacing, these faceless emotions a horizon swell, therein mind is open and sustaining, contained almost, evaporating as lingering, rolling intermittent surge, time underneath, a felicitous current upholding fear, a physics of misguided shaming, vows of an ongoing machination, a raking trouble; who goes there behind these infinite encounters of an unpredictable charge, of an absence that yet zero is never still, though upon the slightest hint of a touch it feigns, in anticipation of fright or flight, to come to a full stop here.

THE BODILY PRESS
bodilypress.bandcamp.com
www.bodilypress.com
@thebodilypress